SCIENCE **HORIZONS**

Space

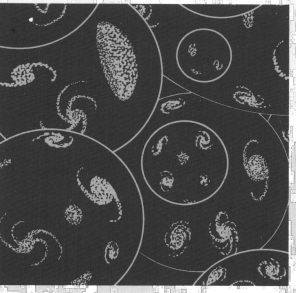

**ROBERT
SNEDDEN**

Chelsea House Publishers
New York • Philadelphia

First published in Great Britain in 1995 by
Belitha Press Limited, 31 Newington Green, London N16 9PU

Editor: Simon de Pinna
Designer: Guy Callaby
Consultant: Bob Kibble
Picture research: Image Select
Cover illustration: Neil Leslie
Other illustrations: Kevin Lyles (8-9, 18 and
28), Chris West (11), David Pugh (22-23 and
41) and Guy Callaby (13, 21, 31, 34 and 42)

Picture acknowledgments
Ancient Art and Architecture: 9, 15 top, 22.
Ann Ronan/Image Select 4-5, 5 bottom, 6, 7, 8 top,
10 top, 10 (background) bottom, 12, 15 bottom,
16 top, middle and bottom, 16-17 top, 19,
19 background, 20, 22, bottom, 25 top, 26 middle,
28-29, 29 top, 34-35, 38-39.
AT & T Bell Laboratories: 39
AKG Berlin: 16 bottom, 17 bottom, 36, 37.
Hulton Deutsch: 38.
Images Colour Library: 5 top, 6 background, 7 top,
21 bottom, 26-27 bottom, 40.
Science Photo Library: 8, 14, 15 middle, 25 bottom,
26 top left, 26 top right, 30, 32, 33, 40 top,
41, 42 bottom.

First printing
1 3 5 7 9 8 6 4 2

Manfactured in China

Library of Congress Cataloging-in-Publication Data
Snedden, Robert.
    Space / Robert Snedden.
        p.   cm. — (Science horizons)
    Includes index.
    ISBN 0-7910-3029-6. — ISBN 0-7910-3033-4 (pbk.)
    1. Astronomy—Juvenile literature. [1. Astronomy.]   I. Title.
    II. Series: Snedden, Robert.   Science horizons.
    QB46.S688   1995
    520—dc20   94-41166
                                              CIP
                                               AC

Contents

CHAPTER ONE

Highway to the unknown

Astronomy, the study of all that lies beyond the Earth's atmosphere, may be the most ancient of the sciences. Its roots lie in our desire to order and understand our lives.

Almost certainly you will have looked up at the night sky at some time or another and thought about what you could see there. In doing so you are no different from the very first people, who must also have looked with wonder on the twinkling, unreachable lights far above their heads. The path towards an understanding of what goes on beyond our tiny planet has been a long one and we haven't reached its end yet. In this book we will retrace that path and try to see where it may be leading. Many great people have walked it, all of them pushing our knowledge of the universe further and further out. Today, we are reaching for the beginning of time and the edge of space.

Heavenly clocks

Before people could write down their ideas they knew about the phases of the moon and the changing positions of the sun and stars. The constant regular motion of the sun, moon and stars were our ancestors' clocks, and because they were so important they were thought to have great powers. For the peoples of many societies these heavenly bodies were gods. Six thousand years

The Milky Way, a band of stars visible in the night sky. This picture was taken from Paris in 1870, before street lighting made the stars more difficult to see.

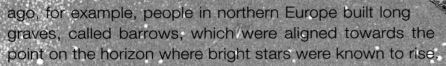

This engraving from a temple in Egypt shows how the Ancient Egyptians divided the night sky into different constellations.

ago, for example, people in northern Europe built long graves, called barrows, which were aligned towards the point on the horizon where bright stars were known to rise.

The positions of the stars guided people in their day-to-day lives. Science and religion were linked in the ancient world and an astronomer-priest was a powerful man in his society. By closely observing the sky he could appear to foretell the future. When the star Sirius rose in the east just before dawn, for example, the Ancient Egyptians knew that the River Nile was about to flood. If these things happened when the stars were in the right positions, could it be because it was the stars that *caused* them to happen? It was from such notions that the art of **astrology** came into being. Modern astronomers believe there is no scientific basis for astrology: the planets and the stars have no influence on life on Earth. Yet still a surprising number of people make time to read their horoscopes in the daily newspapers. Some beliefs die hard.

Astrology is not the only discredited belief about the universe, although some ideas persisted for better reasons. We no longer believe that the Earth is at the center of the universe, or that it floats on an endless ocean, or that the stars are fixed to the inside of a sphere. Yet perhaps some of the ideas that are now being put forward to explain the universe are no less extraordinary.

The peoples of the ancient world divided the stars into groups called constellations, which reminded them of gods and heroes. This is the hunter Orion.

CHAPTER TWO

The celestial spheres

For thousands of years stargazers and astronomers have made maps and imagined models of the heavens.

The first astronomers whose records we can still find were the Ancient Egyptians and the Chinese. In 1990 a Chinese star map painted on the roof of a tomb was uncovered. The map is over 2,000 years old and may have been painted by the emperor's court astrologer. Although the Chinese were first-class observers they were not scientists. They did not attempt to explain what they saw. The Chinese saw events in the natural world mirroring those in human society; both were intricate and could not be predicted in advance. They believed that nature is far too complicated for us to understand and it is pointless to try. The Chinese universe was a magical place in which the idea that nature is governed by general laws played no part.

Astronomy and religion

Although observations of the sky played a big part in their lives, the Egyptian astronomers took us no further towards an

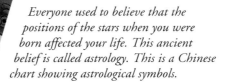

Everyone used to believe that the positions of the stars when you were born affected your life. This ancient belief is called astrology. This is a Chinese chart showing astrological symbols.

understanding of what moved the universe. They may have produced one of the most advanced calendars in the ancient world, more than 4,500 years ago, but their view of the universe was based on religion rather than on science. The Ancient Egyptians believed the sun was the god Ra crossing the sky in his rowboat, for example.

In the Near East the Babylonians, living in what is now Iraq, drew up a remarkable series of astrological charts over 3,000 years ago. Among them were detailed lists of the rising and setting times for the planet Venus. Drawing up these lists would have required careful observation over a very long period. Yet the Babylonians were interested in little more than predicting events in the sky so that they could forecast events on Earth. For all its sophistication, Babylonian astronomy had more to do with fortune-telling than science. For the first genuine attempts at a scientific, reasoned explanation for what was happening above their heads, we have to turn to the Ancient Greeks.

This Egyptian chart was used to help astrologers make their predictions.

A medieval artist's idea of how Thales might have looked. Thales was one of the first people to try and explain in scientific terms how the universe worked.

What is the universe made of?

The Greek philosopher Thales lived in the town of Miletus, in what is now Turkey, around 600 BC. He is generally credited as being the first person we know who tried to answer the question "What is the universe made of?" without giving an answer that depended on the supernatural. His solution was, to us, unexpected. The universe, Thales said, is made of water and the Earth floats in an infinite ocean. He must have been aware of, and influenced by, the beliefs of the Babylonians and Egyptians. Water was vital to the peoples of the ancient world and it should be no surprise that it was given such an important role.

Thales' pupil Anaximander attempted to draw a map of the whole Earth. It had long been observed that the stars seen from the northern hemisphere appear to rotate around Polaris, the North Star. Anaximander imagined the sky as spheres surrounding the Earth, with the stars on an inner sphere and the sun and moon on an outer one. He disagreed with Thales about what the universe was made of, asking where the water was in things that were hot and dry. Instead, he said that all things arose from a **fundamental essence**, which was featureless, and unlike anything else.

Other thinkers tried to describe the universe in terms of what was familiar to them. At various

This photograph, taken during one night, shows how stars appear to move. This movement is caused by the spinning of the Earth, not by movement of the stars themselves.

Thales believed the Earth to be either a disk or a short cylinder, floating on a watery ocean.

times it was said to be made of air, of earth, of fire, as well as of water. Empedocles, who lived in Acragas on the island of Sicily, around 450 BC, put these ideas together and said that all things were a mixture of air, earth, fire and water. Empedocles is credited as being the first to suggest, after examining a **meteor**, that the Earth and stars are made from the same materials.

The music of the spheres

One of the greatest Greek thinkers was Plato. His ideas influenced thought long after his death. Plato was born in Athens around 427 BC. He declared that the heavens were perfect and so the stars and planets must move in "perfect curves on perfect solids," circles around spheres, in other words. He believed that the spheres made music as they turned, an idea that persisted for many centuries.

However, Plato's **celestial spheres** did not fit what most people actually observed. Sometimes the planets did funny things; they looped backwards in their paths before turning back and carrying on in the first direction again. How was this to be explained? The Greeks were reluctant to give up what seemed a good idea. The astronomer Eudoxus came up with a complex scheme that involved spheres moving within spheres within yet more spheres, all rotating in slightly different directions.

Plato, one of the greatest of the Ancient Greek thinkers. He believed that the planets moved in perfect circles.

9

Ptolemy (on the right), who wrote a book called the Almagest *around AD 100. It presented a picture of the universe with the Earth at the center and everything else turning around it.*

Ptolemy imagined that the universe consisted of concentric spheres revolving around the Earth. In Ptolemy's model each of the five planets known at that time, as well as the moon and the sun, is fixed to one of the spheres, with the stars attached to the outermost sphere. He thought that each heavenly body rotated on an orbit called an epicycle, except for the Earth, which did not move.

Around 260 BC the astronomer Aristarchus came up with an idea that was way ahead of its time. The Earth wasn't the center of the universe at all, he said; everything went around the sun. This explained the observations that had been made of the planets, without having to resort to Eudoxus' complex theories. Since the stars appeared not to move, apart from motion that was due to the Earth rotating beneath them, Aristarchus reasoned that this must be because they are infinitely far away. These notions seemed much too far-fetched for the people of the time and his ideas were rejected.

Belief in celestial spheres, with the Earth at the center, persisted. Other schemes were put forward, such as having the planets orbit the sun, which in turn orbited the Earth, carrying the planets with it. Around AD 100 a book was published that summarized astronomical thinking up until then. This was the *Almagest*, written by the astronomer Ptolemy.

Ptolemy's universe looked like this: the Earth was at the center and around it, in increasing order of distance, were the moon, Mercury, Venus, the sun, Mars, Jupiter and Saturn. The planets were attached to little spheres and moved in circles called **epicycles**. The little spheres were attached to larger spheres surrounding the Earth. The stars were fixed to an eighth sphere surrounding the others. It has to be said that this system worked! It could be used to predict accurately where the planets would be in the sky and, more importantly, it gave reasons why.

Astronomy seemed to be more or less stuck after this. It would be another 1,400 years before more accurate observations made it necessary to find a better explanation.

1 *The Earth*
2 *The moon*
3 *Mercury*
4 *Venus*
5 *The sun*
6 *Mars*
7 *Jupiter*
8 *Saturn*
9 *The stars*

CHAPTER THREE

Revolutions

In the sixteenth and seventeenth centuries people began to question the accepted ideas about the universe.

A coin showing a portrait of the Polish astronomer Copernicus who suggested that the Earth went around the sun.

In 1543 astronomy was kicked out of its long slumber when a book called *On the Revolutions of the Celestial Spheres* was published. Its author, the astronomer Nicolaus Copernicus, was born in Torun, Poland, in 1473. In 1507 it occurred to Copernicus that it would be much easier to work out the positions of the planets if he assumed that the sun was at the center of the universe and that the planets, including the Earth, went around it. As we have seen, this was not entirely a new idea. Aristarchus had suggested it almost 1,800 years earlier. Copernicus began to work out the details of his new system and found that it explained some of the puzzling aspects of planetary movement, such as why some planets occasionally seemed to travel backwards. If the Earth was going around the sun in a smaller orbit than Mars, Jupiter and Saturn, then every so often it would overtake them. They would appear, from our point of view, to be going in reverse.

The Copernican system was much simpler than Ptolemy's and yet Copernicus still believed that the planets must move in perfect circles on solid celestial spheres. This meant that his system had to have some epicycles built in, too. In effect, Copernicus was really adapting the Greek system rather than overthrowing it. Yet this was an important step away from the view of the universe that had held sway for so long.

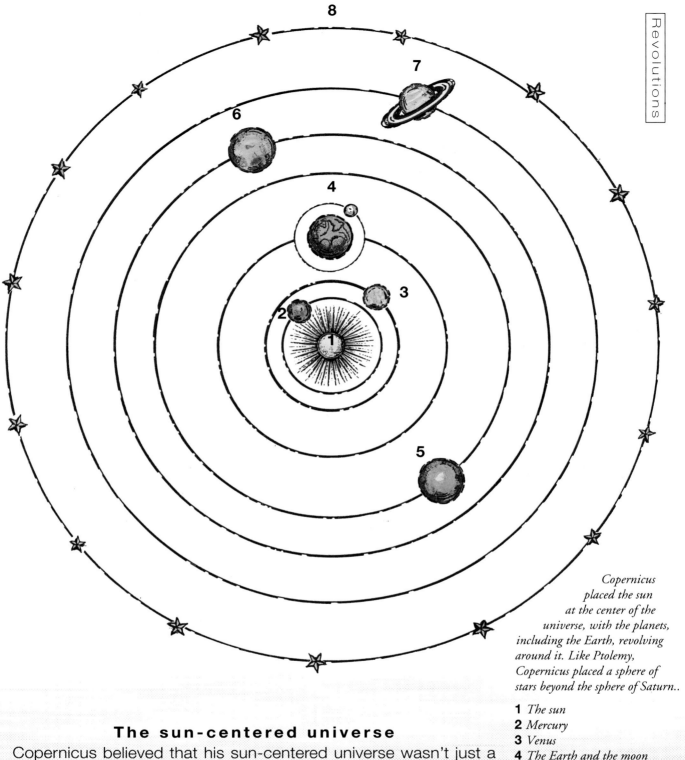

8

7

6

4

3

2

1

5

Copernicus placed the sun at the center of the universe, with the planets, including the Earth, revolving around it. Like Ptolemy, Copernicus placed a sphere of stars beyond the sphere of Saturn..

1 *The sun*
2 *Mercury*
3 *Venus*
4 *The Earth and the moon*
5 *Mars*
6 *Jupiter*
7 *Saturn*
8 *The stars*

The sun-centered universe

Copernicus believed that his sun-centered universe wasn't just a device for simplifying calculations. He thought the universe really was like that. Pause for a moment and try to put yourself in the position of someone hearing this idea for the first time. For thousands of years humanity had believed itself to be at the center of creation, and suddenly along had come someone who

Tycho Brahe was probably the greatest astronomer of the age before the telescope.

dared to suggest it wasn't so. Unsurprisingly, it was not a popular suggestion, especially with the church.

No one at that time willingly made an enemy of the church, and Copernicus was careful to restrict the circulation of his ideas. He eventually agreed to publish his *Revolutions*, dedicating it to Pope Paul III. When the book was being printed, a minister named Andreas Osiander added an introduction without Copernicus' approval. In it he said that these new ideas need not be considered as true! Copernicus had no opportunity to demand a correction; it is said that he received a bound copy of the book when he was on his deathbed. It was several decades before people discovered that Copernicus hadn't written the introduction.

The new star

For some time nothing changed. Many astronomers carried on working with the old, familiar system. Yet word of the new Copernican model began to spread. The idea that the sun goes around the Earth and that the planets go around the sun was revived by the Danish astronomer Tycho Brahe (1546–1601). Tycho was one of the greatest astronomers of the days before the invention of the telescope. His reputation was made when he

Tycho's observatory. From here he made many detailed observations of the night sky.

published, in 1573, a short book entitled *De Nova Stella*, which means "On the new star." In it Tycho described his observations of a new star that had appeared the previous year. We now know that this was not a new star at all, but a star that had suddenly exploded and increased enormously in brightness. Ever since, exploding stars have been called **novas**.

In 1577 Tycho made some detailed observations of a comet that appeared in that year. The Ancient Greeks had believed that comets moved through the Earth's atmosphere, but Tycho showed that the comet he had seen must be further away than the moon. It also seemed that the comet did not move on a circular path, but followed a route that took it through the celestial spheres. As a firm believer in the old system, Tycho was not very comfortable with this. In an attempt to explain the comet's behavior, he suggested that all planets, except for the Earth, moved around the sun.

Towards the end of his life, Tycho heard of the work of Johannes Kepler (1571–1630), one of the first firm supporters of the Copernican view. Tycho was so impressed by the quality of Kepler's work that he invited him to be his assistant. Kepler accepted the position, a decision that was of great importance to the development of astronomy.

A supernova, or exploding star (circled in yellow), seen in a distant galaxy.

Johannes Kepler, an astronomer who studied with Tycho and used his observations to produce a set of laws, or rules, to explain the movements of the planets.

Through the telescope

In Italy the great scientist Galileo Galilei (1564–1642) had come to believe in Copernicus' ideas and, in fact, exchanged letters with Kepler on the subject. Galileo's great contribution to astronomy began in 1609 when he got hold of a copy of an invention from Holland, the telescope. By modern standards Galileo's telescopes were modest instruments, magnifying a mere 20 to 30 times. Even so, when he pointed his telescope upwards, what he saw must have astounded him.

Galileo discovered that the moon had mountains and that there were spots on the sun. The heavens were not as perfect as the church had taught. Through his telescope the planets appeared to be little disks, but the stars remained points of light. Galileo concluded from this that the stars must be much further away than the planets. He also discovered that there were many more stars than could be seen with the unaided eye. Most sensationally of all, on the night of January 7, 1610, he discovered the moons of Jupiter, proof that not all bodies in space circle the Earth. Jupiter and its moons were like the solar system in miniature. He also

Galileo, who used the new invention of the telescope to explore the night sky.

Galileo was one of the first people to see the mountains and craters on the surface of the moon.

Galileo's drawings of the planet Saturn. His telescope wasn't quite good enough to show him that what he saw were rings around the planet.

The most accurate maps made of the moon are assembled from images taken by orbiting space probes.

saw, for the first time, that the planet Venus had phases, just like the moon. This proved that Venus shone by reflecting the light of the sun. Galileo published his findings in a book called *Starry Messenger.* Kepler received a copy and wrote in support of Galileo's findings. Galileo took his telescope to Rome to demonstrate his discoveries to high-ranking members of the church and succeeded in winning many of them over, but not enough of them. In February 1616 he was ordered to give up any ideas that the Earth moved. A week later, Copernicus' *On the Revolutions of the Celestial Spheres* was placed on the Catholic church's list of forbidden books. It stayed there until 1835.

Tycho's records

In Prague Kepler, without the benefit of a telescope, had come to some far-reaching conclusions of his own. As Tycho Brahe's successor, he had gained access to the great astronomer's huge collection of accurate observations following Tycho's death on October 24, 1601. Kepler set out on a careful study of Tycho's records, concentrating on those for the planet Mars. He realized that it just wasn't possible to fit the observations of the planet's movements to the idea that it moved in a perfect circle. Mars was moving in a flattened circle, called an ellipse.

Galileo kept careful records of his observations over several months.

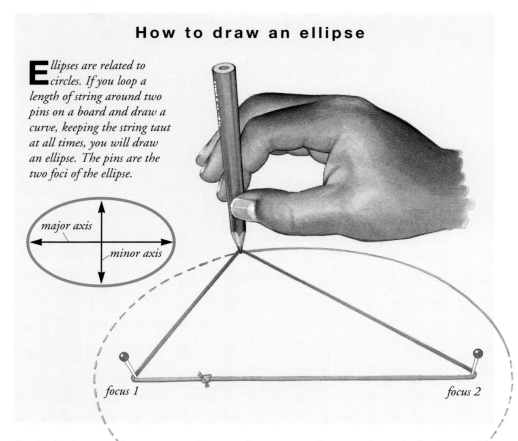

How to draw an ellipse

Ellipses are related to circles. If you loop a length of string around two pins on a board and draw a curve, keeping the string taut at all times, you will draw an ellipse. The pins are the two foci of the ellipse.

major axis

minor axis

focus 1

focus 2

A circle has only one center and every point on the circle is at the same distance from the center; the diameter of the circle is the same length wherever you measure it. The diameter of an **ellipse**, on the other hand, varies according to where it is measured. The longest diameter is called the major **axis** and the shortest is the minor axis. On the major axis are two points called foci (singular: **focus**), which lie at an equal distance from the center of the ellipse. Kepler discovered that the orbit of Mars fitted an ellipse as exactly as he could work out. At one of the foci of his ellipse was the sun.

Kepler's laws

When he looked at the orbits of the other planets, Kepler found that they also moved in ellipses, with the sun at one focus. This led him to his first law of planetary motion: the planets move in ellipses with the sun at one focus. In 1609, the year Galileo got his first telescope, Kepler published his work in a book called *New Astronomy.* It also included his second law, dealing with the **velocity** of the planets as they travel around the sun. This law states that an imaginary line joining the sun and a planet moves over equal areas in equal times, as the planet moves in its orbit. The closer a planet is to the sun, the faster it moves.

Kepler had finally put an end to the perfect circles of the heavens. Galileo sent Kepler a telescope and he saw for himself the moons of Jupiter. Kepler gave them the name **satellites**, after a word describing people who surround a more powerful person. The name stuck and we still use it today to describe a small body in orbit around a larger one. Kepler tried out his laws on Jupiter's moons and found that they, too, were moving in ellipses. In 1619 Kepler published a third law, relating the distance of a planet from the sun to the time it takes to complete its orbit.

Kepler tried to work out what the force might be that was controlling the movements of the planets. Not surprisingly, he thought the sun might have something to do with it, but how was the force transmitted? Kepler thought it might be a form of magnetism: William Gilbert (1540–1603), the physician to Queen Elizabeth I, had recently demonstrated that the Earth acted like a giant bar magnet, but he was unable to produce a satisfactory explanation. That would come some 50 years later from Isaac Newton and his famous work on **gravity**.

The title page of Galileo's famous book, Concerning the Two Chief World Systems, *in which he set out the differences between the views of Ptolemy and Copernicus.*

Kepler's great work did not get the approval it deserved. In 1632 Galileo published his *Dialogue Concerning the Two Chief World Systems*, setting out in the form of an imaginary conversation the differences between the views of Ptolemy and Copernicus. There was no doubt that Galileo's sympathies were with Copernicus, yet nowhere did he mention Kepler's findings, which backed up this view. The church disapproved strongly of Galileo's views and, under threat of torture, he was forced to withdraw his support for Copernicus.

There was no turning back, however. The belief in an Earth-centered universe would have to be abandoned, despite the efforts of the church. The scientific revolution that Copernicus had started was not so easily stopped.

Io, one of the moons of Jupiter, photographed from a space probe passing close by. Galileo was the first person to discover that Jupiter had moons.

CHAPTER FOUR

The universal force

The scientific laws that govern the movements of bodies in space have their origin in the work of a great seventeenth-century scientist, Isaac Newton.

Isaac Newton was born in Woolsthorpe, Lincolnshire, on Christmas Day 1642, the year Galileo died. The story has often been told of Newton sitting in his mother's garden on a moonlit night. He was disturbed by the sound of an apple falling from a nearby tree. The thought came to him, "Why doesn't the moon fall to Earth, like the apple?" It took genius to come up with the answer; the moon *is* falling. The force that holds the moon in orbit around the Earth is the same force that attracts the apple to the ground. Newton reasoned that, in fact, the moon is falling *around* the Earth. It wasn't enough simply to have such an insight, however, it had to be proved by calculation.

Sir Isaac Newton, who succeeded in explaining why all objects, from a falling apple to the planets traveling around the sun, move as they do.

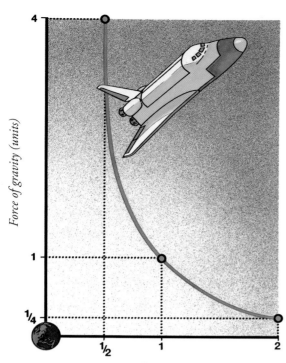

Force of gravity (units)

4

1

¼

½   1   2

Distance from center of Earth (units)

This shows how the inverse-square law links distance with gravitational force. A spacecraft at a distance of 1 unit from the Earth is attracted with a force of 1 unit. If the spacecraft moves away to a distance of two units, the gravitational pull from the Earth is a quarter what it was. On the other hand, if the space-craft approaches to within half a unit of the Earth, the force of gravity increases to 4 units.

The diminishing force

Newton was aware of Kepler's laws, which had by then been accepted by scientists. He knew that any explanation he came up with for the motion of both the moon and the apple would have to explain Kepler's ideas, too. Newton proposed that the rate at which an object falls depends on the strength of the **gravitational force** acting on it. He calculated that the size of the force acting between two objects changes according to what is known as the **inverse-square law**. As the distance between the objects increases, the force decreases by the distance squared, or multiplied by itself. This means that if the distance doubles, the force is a quarter of what it was; if the distance triples, the force is cut to a ninth.

To compare the rate at which the apple fell with that of the moon, Newton had to discover how much further away from the center of the Earth the moon was than the apple. There was not much information available; there was no accurate measurement of the Earth's size, for example, and the results of his calculations did not agree with what he observed. Newton also had to create a whole new branch of mathematics, the **calculus**, to deal with the numbers involved.

It was 1679 before Newton returned to the problem. His great scientific rival, Robert Hooke, had boasted

that he could prove mathematically that, since the planets moved in ellipses, the force pulling them towards the sun would vary according to the inverse-square law. Newton set about doing the calculations himself. In 1684 the astronomer Edmund Halley, to whom we shall return shortly, tiring of Hooke's continual boasting, went to Newton and asked him if he could prove Hooke's idea. Newton replied that he had done so five years earlier but had mislaid the papers! At Halley's urging Newton did the work again. He showed that if an object in space obeys Kepler's second law then it is being acted upon by a force of attraction, and that if this force obeys the inverse-square law, the path the object follows will be an ellipse.

Gravity and motion

Halley persuaded Newton to produce a book setting out his new ideas concerning motion and gravity. After 18 months of hard work Newton published, in 1687, a book that many believe to be the greatest work of science ever written. This was his *Mathematical Principles of Natural Philosophy*, usually referred to as the *Principia*, from its Latin title. Within it Newton put forward a vision of the universe in which all events took place against a background of infinite space and smoothly flowing time.

Building on Galileo's experiments with moving objects and Kepler's work on the movements of the planets, Newton set out his three laws of motion. These say that:

(1) a moving body will continue to move in the same direction and at the same speed unless something diverts it;

(2) any change in the speed or direction of a moving object depends on the size of the force acting on the object, divided by the mass of the object;

(3) for every action there is an equal and opposite reaction.

Edmund Halley, who used Newton's laws of motion to calculate the path of the comet that was named after him. He correctly predicted that it would be seen again in 76 years time.

The arrival of Halley's Comet has been recorded at least 29 times, going back to 239 BC. In its most recent visit to the Earth's neighborhood, in March 1986, the spacecraft Giotto photographed the comet and analyzed its tail. The comet seems to consist of ice and dust, as first suggested by the American astronomer Fred Whipple in 1950, in his "dirty snowball" model. After passing beyond the orbit of Neptune, Halley's Comet will eventually return in the year 2061.

Newton's theory of gravity, the force that attracts all objects to each other, says that the size of the force is proportional to the objects' masses multiplied together. It also states that the force decreases as the distance between the objects increases, according to the inverse-square law.

Gravity and the laws of motion apply to all objects, whether they be apples falling to Earth or planets orbiting the sun. Isaac Newton's laws provided the first real explanation for Kepler's laws of planetary motion. Using Newton's laws, Edmund Halley calculated that a comet that appeared in 1682 had followed the same path as a comet seen in 1531 and 1607. He suggested that it was the same comet returning each time, and predicted that it would be seen again in 1758. Sure enough, it did return, and though Halley was not alive to see it, the comet was named after him – Halley's Comet. In time, astronomers would show that Newton's laws could be applied to the whole universe.

A section of the Bayeux Tapestry, telling the story of the Norman invasion of England in 1066. The comet shown here is Halley's Comet on one of its regular visits to the inner solar system.

CHAPTER FIVE

An infinite universe?

During the eighteenth and nineteenth centuries the major challenge to astronomers was to answer questions about the size of the universe.

In 1692, while at Cambridge University, Newton received a letter from the Reverend Richard Bentley. The possibility that the universe was infinite in size had been discussed for over a hundred years and Bentley said that if this were so then every part of the universe would feel the pull of gravity. Everything in the universe should collapse together.

Newton tried to explain this by saying that if the stars were distributed evenly through space then the force of gravity between them would be acting equally in all directions. (Although the force of gravity decreases with distance it never disappears.) The universe would be balanced and there would be no collapse. He quickly realized, however, that this solution just would not do. If there were the slightest movement of any star the balance would be lost and everything in the universe would crash together, either in one great pile of stars and planets or in many smaller ones.

Olbers' Paradox

Both Newton and Bentley had made one great error. They had assumed that the stars were stationary. It was Edmund Halley who pointed out, in 1718, that at least three stars, Sirius, Arcturus and Procyon, had shifted from the positions recorded for them on Greek star maps. He concluded that the stars were moving, but because they were so far away the movement only became apparent over many years. The fact that the stars were moving led to the conclusion that they were scattered throughout

Olbers thought that dustclouds in space, such as this one shaped something like the head of a horse, might be concealing stars from our sight.

space and not equal distances apart. It was the motion of the stars that prevented gravity from pulling them all together.

Halley pointed out another problem presented by the idea of an infinite universe. Kepler had written in 1610: "in an infinite universe the stars would fill the heavens." So wherever you looked there would be a star. The entire sky should be shining as brightly as the sun! The fact that it wasn't led Kepler to believe that the universe is not infinitely big. The problem became known as Olbers' **Paradox**, after the German astronomer Heinrich Olbers (1758–1840). Olbers suggested that there must be clouds of dust between the stars that hid some of them from our view. But this solution doesn't work. Eventually, the energy from the stars behind the dustclouds would heat them until they glowed and the sky would still be filled with light. The reason the night sky is dark wouldn't be found for another hundred years.

German astronomer Heinrich Olbers, who asked the question that became known as Olbers' Paradox: "Why is the sky dark at night?"

The Herschels, William, discoverer of the planet Uranus, his sister Caroline, also a skilled astronomer, and William's son John, who carried on his father's work.

Meanwhile, the end of belief in the sphere of fixed stars led astronomers to investigate how the stars were distributed in space. In 1750 the English astronomer Thomas Wright (1711–86) tried to explain the appearance of the Milky Way – a band of light in the night sky. Unfortunately, because of street lights, the Milky Way isn't clearly visible today from our towns and cities; the sky is never dark enough to see it properly. Before the invention of the telescope people thought it was a kind of cloud, but now it had been revealed as a collection of many stars. Wright thought there must be many more stars in the direction of the Milky Way than elsewhere.

Mapping the Milky Way

In the 1780s William Herschel (1738–1822), one of the greatest astronomers of his age, also turned his attention to the Milky Way and the cloud-like **nebulas**, fuzzy patches of light in the night sky. Ptolemy had recorded six or seven in his catalog, but with the advent of the telescope more had been discovered. Herschel set out on a 20-year program of star counting and nebula-spotting. He was greatly helped in this work by his sister Caroline (1750–1848), who not only helped William build his telescopes but was also a skilled astronomer in her own right, discovering eight new comets.

Herschel established his claim to greatness on March 13, 1781. On that night he saw, through his telescope, an object that he knew was not a star. To begin with he thought it was a comet. Other astronomers had trouble confirming the existence of this new object, but Herschel's telescopes were the best available at the time. Eventually, the orbit of the object was calculated. This was no comet that Herschel had discovered but a new planet. He was the first person to do so in recorded history. After much discussion the new planet was named Uranus, though for years it was called "Herschelium" in France, in the astronomer's honor.

In order to draw up a three-dimensional map of the universe, Herschel assumed first, that his telescope was good enough to see to the furthest reaches of the Milky Way, and second, that the stars were distributed regularly within it. There was no way to calculate the distances to the stars at the time and so astronomers were forced to make guesses. After counting stars in well over 3,000 places in the sky, Herschel produced his first chart, in 1785. The universe, he believed, was a great disk of stars with the sun positioned somewhere near the center. The Milky Way was what we could see when we looked out towards the edge of the disk.

A nebula, a huge cloud of gas and dust in space. The radiation from nearby stars makes the gas glow.

The lights from our cities make it difficult to see the fainter lights of the stars in the night sky.

27

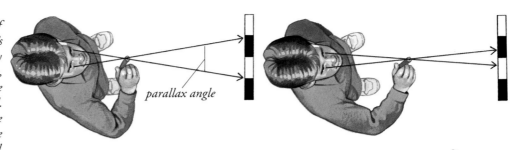

Observing the parallax of a pencil held at arm's length. As you alternately open and close each eye, the pencil appears to move relative to the background. The closer you hold the pencil, the larger the movement of the pencil appears to be. If you know the distance between each eye and the angle of the apparent movement (the parallax angle), you can calculate how far away the pencil is.

parallax angle

The sun could only be placed near the center of the universe, but not exactly there. For Herschel had discovered that the sun, like the other stars, was moving. Almost three centuries before, Copernicus had shown that the Earth could not be at the center of the universe, and now Herschel had said that the sun could not be there either.

For some time after Herschel had drawn up his map of the Milky Way, or the **galaxy** as it was often called (from the Greek word for milk), astronomers got no further in determining the structure of the universe. It was not until 1838 that the first successful measurement of the distance from the Earth to a star was made. In that year Friedrich Bessel (1784–1846), a German astronomer, calculated the distance to the faint star 61 Cygni. He did so by determining its **parallax**.

Parallax

Parallax is a measure of how an object appears to shift in position against a more distant background, when viewed from different angles. Try it for yourself. Hold up a finger and, with one eye closed, line up your finger with a tree outside or a book on a shelf. Now look at the finger through the other eye. It will appear in a different position against the background. The amount it seems to move depends on the distance between the finger and your eye. The closer your finger, the further it will move. This effect is called parallax. To calculate the distance to a star Bessel had to make careful measurements of its change in position relative to two fainter and, he assumed, more distant stars, as seen from opposite ends of the Earth's orbit. His answer was a surprise – 61 Cygni was 35 trillion miles (56 trillion kilometers) away, much further than anyone had guessed. Such large numbers are difficult to handle and astronomers soon began to use another unit of measurement – the **light-year**. This is the distance light travels in one year – 5.878 trillion miles (9.46 trillion kilometers) – making the distance to 61 Cygni roughly six light-years.

William Herschel's map of the galaxy, drawn in 1785. He made two mistakes in drawing this chart, believing that the stars were spread evenly across the sky and that his telescope was powerful enough to see to the edge of the galaxy.

Measuring the distances to stars was difficult and required very accurate instruments. By 1900 fewer than 300 distances were known, still far too few to build up a three-dimensional picture of the whole universe. By this time, however, astronomers had a new tool at their disposal – the camera. Photographic film could be made that was more sensitive than the human eye and images of very faint objects could be captured. From 1878 onwards Jacobus Kapteyn (1851–1922) spent 12 years measuring the positions of stars recorded on photographic plates taken by the Scottish astronomer David Gill (1843–1914).

Kapteyn published a catalog of more than 450,000 stars in the sky over the southern hemisphere. From his star counting Kapteyn concluded that the galaxy was shaped like a disk, just as Herschel had thought. He believed it to be 55,000 light-years in diameter and 11,000 light-years thick.

Star streams

Kapteyn went on to study the motion of the stars. Until then, astronomers thought that the stars moved around randomly, but Kapteyn discovered that the stars divided into two streams: three-fifths of them were moving in one direction and the remainder were moving in the opposite direction. Kapteyn could not explain these results and it was a student of his, Jan Oort (1900–92), who eventually provided the answer – the galaxy is spinning around its center.

Oort said that, since the galaxy is not a solid disk, all the stars in it do not rotate at the same speed. Those nearer the center move faster than those towards the outside. The stars closer to the center of the galaxy than the sun are going faster and overtake us, while those further out fall behind us as we overtake them. Kapteyn's two star streams represent the central stars moving ahead and the outermost stars falling behind. The sun, for example, takes 200 million years to complete one circuit of the galaxy.

Astronomers near Paris, towards the end of the nineteenth century, built up star charts by photographing the night sky.

CHAPTER SIX

Further out and further back

At last, by the beginning of the twentieth century, astronomers had a reliable way of measuring the vast stellar distances.

Henrietta Leavitt, whose work on the brightness of stars led to a method for calculating the distances to the stars.

In the 1910s Henrietta Leavitt (1868–1921), one of a group of pioneering American women astronomers, discovered that the brightness of a group of stars called **Cepheid variables** was related to the time each star took to go through a complete cycle from bright to dim and back to bright again. (A variable star is one that changes in brightness over a regular period.) The brighter the star, the longer it took to go through its cycle. A simple calculation, based on how bright the star appeared to be, allowed Leavitt to work out the star's distance from the Earth.

Then, in 1914, Harlow Shapley (1885–1972), another American, began a study of collections of stars called **globular clusters**. These consist of between ten thousand and a million stars, including some Cepheid variables, in a roughly spherical arrangement. By using Leavitt's method he discovered that a typical globular cluster was some 50,000 light-years away; in 1916 he found one that was almost 100,000 light-years distant. To take account of measurements such as these, the universe would have to be ten times bigger than the size Kapteyn had calculated. Shapley also discovered that the globular clusters were not evenly spread across the sky and he decided that the center of the galaxy must lie where these clusters were most

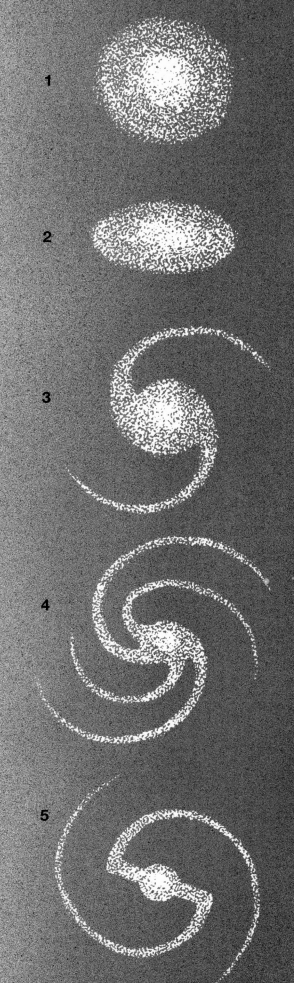

Galaxies are classified by their shapes. Elliptical galaxies can be nearly circular, while others are thin ellipses. Spiral galaxies can have two arms or many, like our own Milky Way, or there may be a line of stars, called a bar, running through the central nucleus of the galaxy.

1 circular
2 elliptical
3 two-armed spiral
4 four-armed spiral
5 barred spiral

dense. Shapley's careful observations led him to the conclusion that the sun wasn't at the center of the Milky Way but was some way out towards the edge. The Earth seemed to be taking up a place in the universe that was less and less important.

Scientists had suspected for some time that at least some nebulas were made up of collections of very distant stars. The question was whether or not they were part of the Milky Way. In 1913 photographic evidence pointed towards the Milky Way being spiral-shaped, and so were many of the nebulas, but people thought these were just smaller patterns within the larger pattern of the Milky Way.

Beyond the Milky Way

Most people, including Shapley, thought that everything in the universe was contained within the Milky Way and that there was nothing else beyond it. Others were considering a different possibility. In 1914, the American astronomer Heber Curtis had described the spiral nebulas as being "inconceivably distant galaxies or universes of stars." The breakthrough came when astronomers found evidence of novas on the photographs they took of nebulas. The novas were far less bright than would have been expected had they been inside the Milky Way. Curtis estimated that they must be a hundred times more distant, and therefore far outside the galaxy.

So who was right? Shapley said the spiral nebulas were fairly small and inside the galaxy. Curtis said they were big enough to be considered as galaxies in their own right and lay far beyond the galaxy. In 1920 the two men met to hold a debate on the size of the universe, but they came to no clear conclusion.

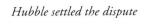

Hubble settled the dispute

between Shapley and Curtis

when he discovered variable stars

inside the Andromeda galaxy,

but he underestimated their distance

by over 1.5 million light-years.

Edwin Hubble, who showed for the first time that there are galaxies outside our own and found the first evidence that the universe is expanding.

The matter was settled in 1923 when Edwin Hubble (1889–1953), an American astronomer, using the most powerful telescope in the world at that time, managed to make out stars in the Andromeda nebula. Hubble went on to show that some of the stars were variables and that their distance could be calculated using Leavitt's findings. He estimated the distance to the Andromeda nebula to be 800,000 light-years, far beyond the galaxy. Science had to wait 20 years before it was discovered that Hubble had underestimated the distance to Andromeda, which is, in fact, two million light-years away.

Hubble found that other nebulas are even further away, some over a trillion light-years distant. The universe is vast beyond anyone's power to comprehend and contains countless trillions of galaxies. In 1929 Hubble looked at the velocities of different galaxies and discovered that the speed at which a galaxy is moving away from us depends on how distant it is. The further away it is from us, the faster a galaxy is moving. Hubble thought that the best explanation for this was that the universe is expanding.

The Andromeda galaxy, a giant spiral galaxy similar in shape to our own Milky Way galaxy. It is over 2 million light-years away but is still one of the closest to us.

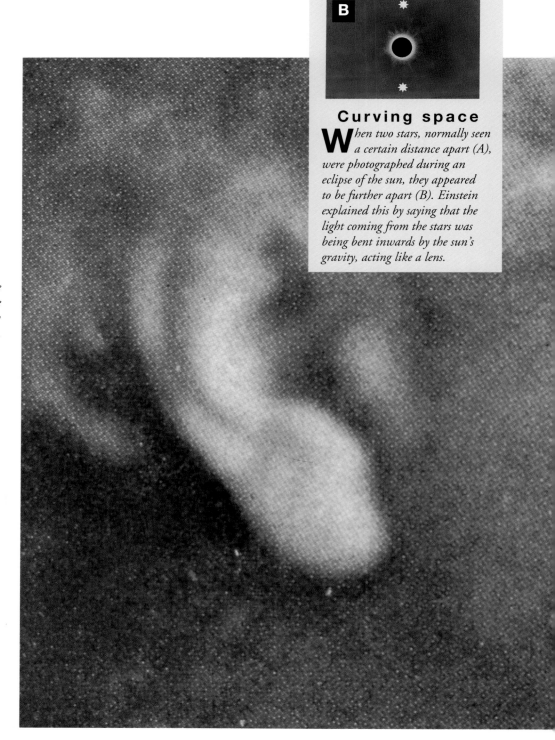

Curving space

When two stars, normally seen a certain distance apart (A), were photographed during an eclipse of the sun, they appeared to be further apart (B). Einstein explained this by saying that the light coming from the stars was being bent inwards by the sun's gravity, acting like a lens.

Albert Einstein, whose relativity theories made scientists rethink the way they saw the universe.

Einstein

A few years earlier, Albert Einstein (1879–1955) had published his relativity theories – the Special Theory in 1905 and the General Theory in 1915. These theories radically changed the way we look at the universe. According to Einstein, for example, gravity was not a force acting between bodies, but a distortion in space, caused by the bodies in it. He said that objects pull the space around them out of shape; the bigger the object the more space curves around it. A smaller object, such as a spacecraft, approaching a larger object, such as a planet, would appear to fall towards it. This wouldn't happen because it was being pulled, but because the path it followed through space was curved towards the planet. Gravity is curved space!

In 1919 the idea of curved space was tested during an **eclipse** of the sun. Einstein had predicted that light traveling towards us from a star would appear to bend as it passed through the strongly curved space close to the sun. It would only be possible to make such an observation during an eclipse, because otherwise the light of the sun would drown out the starlight. When the photographs were developed they showed that Einstein had been right, the stars near the sun did appear to shift.

Einstein's General Theory also said that the universe had to be either expanding or contracting. He reasoned that a static universe could not exist, because the curving of space by all the galaxies would cause everything to collapse together. If the universe was neither static nor collapsing it had to be expanding. Einstein himself, like many others, could not accept this idea. His worry was that, if the universe was expanding, it had to be expanding from somewhere. Long ago, the universe must have started out from a single point, containing all space and time. At this point, called a **singularity**, all the rules we have for understanding the universe would break down. It would be impossible to work out what came before. Einstein thought this was a nonsensical idea. To avoid it he introduced a "**cosmological constant**" into his equations, a mysterious force that counterbalanced gravity and prevented the universe from expanding or contracting.

Hubble's discovery of the relationship between how far away galaxies are and their velocities could not be disputed, however. Einstein admitted that he had been wrong, saying the cosmological constant was the biggest blunder of his life. Now the question was, if the universe was expanding, what was causing it to expand?

Expansion of the super-atom

The first to suggest a possible answer was Georges Henri Lemaître (1894–1966), a Belgian priest and astronomer. Between 1927 and 1933 he put forward his idea of the "**primordial atom**." He suggested that, far back in time, all the material in the universe had been in the form of a single super-atom. According to Lemaître this primordial atom started to divide over and over again, eventually forming all the matter in the universe. He tried to interest Einstein in the idea. Einstein was unimpressed at first, but later came to

The Belgian astronomer Georges Henri Lemaître (on the right) put forward the idea that the universe began as a single super-atom that later expanded. Einstein (on the left) was skeptical at first but later came to believe it to be a good idea.

believe that the idea was a good one. Many others came to share his opinion, but it would be another 30 years before proof was found.

A cooling universe

Then, after the Second World War, a Russian-born scientist named George Gamow (1904–68) suggested that, in the beginning, the universe was made up of a substance he called **ylem**. This was an extremely hot "soup" of atomic particles, at a temperature of trillions of degrees. For some reason the ylem began to expand and break up. As it expanded it cooled, as the energy it contained was spread over a larger and larger volume of space. Eventually it had cooled enough for all the matter we now see in the universe to form. In 1948 Ralph Alpher (born 1921) and Robert Herman (born 1914) published a scientific paper in which they predicted that **radiation** from the early beginnings of the universe should still exist. They calculated that this **cosmic background radiation**, as it was called, would have a temperature of about minus 450°F (minus 268°C). It was the last faint glow of the unimaginable explosion that gave birth to the universe. Unfortunately, in the 1940s, there was no way to detect such low temperatures and so the prediction was more or less forgotten for the next 20 years.

In 1950, soon after Gamow published his theory, the English astronomer Fred Hoyle (born 1915) gave a radio talk. Hoyle is a fierce opponent of the idea of an expanding universe, believing it to exist in what he calls a "**steady state**." He mocked Gamow's ideas, describing them as a **big bang**. Hoyle had meant the phrase to be insulting, but it stuck in the public's imagination and from then on the beginning of the universe was called the big bang.

For almost 20 years arguments raged between Hoyle's supporters, who believed that the universe had always

Cambridge astronomer Martin Ryle, who helped to develop the new techniques of radio astronomy.

existed and had no beginning in time, and those who were believers in the big bang theory. The end for the steady state theory came from the new and expanding field of **radio astronomy**.

The birth of radio astronomy

Radio astrononomy was discovered by accident when, in the 1930s, Karl Jansky (1905–50), an American radio engineer, detected **radio waves** coming from the center of the galaxy. Scientists soon discovered that there were many other radio sources in the sky. These are not broadcasts from intelligent life forms elsewhere in the universe. Radio waves are, in fact, similar to light waves, but they carry less energy. The sun, for example, gives off energy in the form of invisible radio waves, as well as light and heat.

In the 1950s the Cambridge radio astronomer Martin Ryle (1918–84) made a map of the radio sources he had detected above the northern hemisphere. If the steady state theory was correct they should have been distributed evenly through space. However, they were not. The further Ryle looked into space, the more radio galaxies he found. Both the light and the radio waves from distant galaxies have taken trillions of years to reach us, and so we see them as they were in the distant past. Astronomers are not simply looking far away, but far back in time, too. Ryle was detecting galaxies as

Arno Penzias (on the left) and Robert Wilson, who were the first to detect the remains of the big bang.

they were closer in time to the big bang. The fact that there were more of them suggested that the universe had been denser then, with everything closer together. This was tremendous support for the big bang theory.

Evidence for the big bang

In 1964 Arno Penzias (born 1933) and Robert Wilson (born 1936) made the discovery that finally tipped the scales towards the occurrence of a big bang. They were using a radio **antenna** to measure **interference** that might obstruct signals arriving from the satellite Echo 1, which had been launched in 1959. They picked up **microwave radiation**, coming from all areas of the sky, which had a temperature equivalent to about minus 454°F (minus 270°C). Penzias and Wilson had no idea what it was they had observed and so they contacted the **astrophysicist** Robert Dicke (born 1916) to ask his opinion. Dicke knew what the pair had found. He had been planning an experiment to detect the background radiation predicted by Alpher and Herman, and he realized that Penzias and Wilson had unknowingly beaten him to it. Penzias and Wilson had detected the remains of the big bang.

The expanding universe provided the answer to Olbers' Paradox. When we look up into the blackest regions of the sky we are looking back to a time when the stars had not yet formed.

Karl Jansky and the radio aerial with which he first detected radio waves from space.

CHAPTER SEVEN

Jocelyn Bell, who discovered the first pulsar in November 1967 while she was a student at Cambridge University.

Black holes and inflation

As the search for the edge of the universe has continued, many scientists have been speculating about the origins of the universe – and its future.

The radio telescope at Jodrell Bank in England. Jocelyn Bell discovered pulsars when she examined signals detected by the telescope.

In 1967 Jocelyn Bell, a graduate student at Cambridge University, noticed something unusual while she was studying records from the Jodrell Bank radio telescope. There seemed to be a rapidly pulsing signal coming from a point in the sky. She made careful observations of the signal and found that the pulses were regularly spaced. Within a few months she had found another

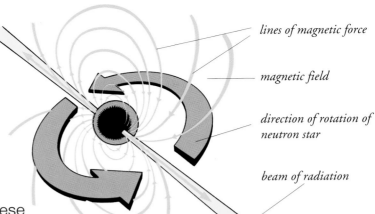

The lighthouse model of a pulsar. A neutron star has a very powerful magnetic field and electrons from the star's surface flow along the lines of force and escape into space, mostly at the magnetic poles. These particles emit radiation, which we detect as pulses when the poles move across our line of sight.

lines of magnetic force

magnetic field

direction of rotation of neutron star

beam of radiation

one. Some people suggested that these might be signals from far-distant intelligent life and they were jokingly referred to as **LGMs** ("little green men").

The American astronomer Thomas Gold (born 1920) suggested that the LGMs were **neutron stars**. Astronomers had speculated for some time on the existence of neutron stars. These would come about when a star stopped burning and its immense gravity pulled it in on itself. All the atomic particles in the star would be crushed together forming a superdense mass. In the center of a neutron star a trillion tons of material are crushed into less than a single cubic inch.

As a star collapses it spins faster and faster, like an ice skater spinning around on the ice by bringing in her arms towards her body. As it gets smaller the star's magnetic field becomes more concentrated and more powerful. **Electrons** within the magnetic field are accelerated to nearly the speed of light and give off radiation from the star's north and south magnetic poles. These beams of radiation are like the light beams from a lighthouse, sweeping around. We can only detect the star when one of the beams is pointing directly towards us. This makes the star appear to pulse as the beam passes the Earth, so these stars were soon given the name **pulsars**.

Black holes

What would happen if a neutron star didn't stop collapsing? In 1928 the Indian astrophysicist Subrahmanyan Chandrasekhar (born 1910) had calculated that if a star was bigger than a certain size, the power of its gravitational force would be greater than the atomic particles in it could resist. It would collapse into a single point, a singularity, bending the space around it so much that nothing, not even light, could escape it. It would become a "**black hole**" in space.

It is impossible to see a black hole directly, but we may be able to see the effect one has on objects near it. Astronomers believe

Subrahmanyan Chandrasekhar, the Indian astrophysicist who calculated that if a star was above a certain size its gravity would make it collapse into a smaller and smaller volume when its nuclear fuel ran out.

41

that some very strong sources of radiation, such as the star Cygnus X-1, are the result of material being sucked into a black hole. The Hubble space telescope has detected evidence of a huge black hole three trillion times more massive than the sun, at the center of a distant galaxy. Astronomers believe that there may be a black hole at the heart of most galaxies, including ours.

In the 1960s the English physicist Stephen Hawking (born 1942) applied the idea of black holes to the whole universe. In 1970 he wrote a scientific paper with Roger Penrose (born 1931) setting out their belief that the universe as we see it must have begun as a singularity that marked the beginning of time. If the universe is like a black hole then everything can be seen as expanding outwards from that first singularity.

Hawking calculated that the universe ought to be expanding at nearly the same rate in all directions – a notion that seemed to be confirmed by the smoothness of the cosmic background radiation discovered by Penzias and Wilson. In fact, the expansion couldn't have been completely smooth; if it had been there would be no large objects, such as planets, stars and galaxies, in the universe. There must have been some areas where there was slightly more matter, in order for the galaxies to form. Scientists set about trying to detect variations in the background radiation, which would prove the early universe had not been smooth.

Voids and ripples

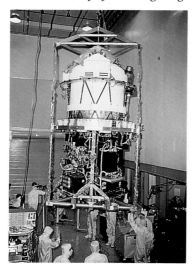

The Cosmic Background Explorer (COBE) satellite being constructed. This produced the first real evidence that the universe did not expand smoothly after the big bang.

We know that the matter in the universe is clumped together in different regions. This "lumpiness" in space exists on a massive scale – astronomers have recently detected a **"Great Wall"** of galaxies, over half a trillion light-years across. But they have also found vast volumes of empty space millions of light-years across, called **voids**. The structure of the universe has even been described as resembling soap bubbles, with galaxies on the surface of the bubbles and nothing in the middle.

In 1992 results from the Cosmic Background Explorer (**COBE**) satellite seemed to show variations in the background radiation for the first time. The results indicated that "**ripples**" had formed in the substance of the universe within 300,000 years of the big bang. This meant that the universe had to be denser than scientists had believed, since the greater the amount of material in the universe, the sooner the ripples would have appeared.

These findings appear to back up the "**inflationary model**" of how the early universe formed. In this idea, according to the particle physicist Alan Guth (born 1947), a tiny fraction of a second after the universe appeared it rapidly increased in size, expanding from a region trillions of times smaller than an atom to about 30 feet (10 meters) across in less than a trillion trillion trillionth of a second. Such a rapid inflation, Guth said, might have spread "imperfections" through space as matter started to appear in the universe, which previously had contained only energy. Each of these imperfections might have become a focus around which stars and galaxies formed. One version of the inflationary model pictures our entire universe as just one among many, an enormous collection of universes stretching on forever.

Since the 1930s astronomers have speculated on the existence of **dark matter**. This is matter that we cannot detect from Earth. If the density of the universe agrees with Guth's model and the COBE satellite results, then perhaps 99 percent of the material in the universe is invisible to us. What is this invisible matter? There have been many guesses but, as yet, no firm answers. Some of it may be in the form of black holes, some as unknown atomic particles, different from anything yet detected. We are continuing to build up a picture of the universe that would have astounded Ptolemy, Galileo and Newton – and the picture is not finished yet.

Glossary

Acceleration *The rate at which an object gains speed or velocity.*

Antenna *Another word for an aerial, the part of a radio that receives radio waves that are being transmitted.*

Astrology *A belief in the power of the stars and planets to influence people's lives.*

Astronomy *The study of everything that lies beyond the Earth's atmosphere.*

Astrophysicist *Someone who studies astrophysics, the study of the physical and chemical changes that take place in planets, stars and galaxies, and other astronomical objects.*

Axis *The line around which an object spins. The Earth's axis runs through it from one pole to the other. An axis is also a line about which an object is symmetrical. An ellipse has a long (major) and a short (minor) axis.*

Big bang *The name given to the theory that all of the matter and energy in the universe originated in a sudden explosion outwards from a single point around 15 trillion years ago.*

Black hole *At the end of its life gravity may cause a massive star to collapse so much that not even light can escape from it. The star becomes invisible, a black hole in space. It may be possible to detect a black hole by the effect* it has on objects near it. Many astronomers believe that the star called Cygnus X-1 is orbiting a black hole.

Calculus *A technique for making calculations involving quantities that are changing continuously. It was developed separately by Sir Isaac Newton and Gottfried Leibniz (1646–1716).*

Celestial spheres *Crystal spheres upon which the planets and stars were thought to move by the Ancient Greeks. There are no spheres, but astronomers today sometimes use the idea of a celestial sphere to describe the positions of objects in space in relation to the Earth.*

Cepheid variable *A type of star that changes in brightness over a regular period of between 1 and 50 days. The first one was discovered in 1784 in the constellation Cepheus. At the beginning of the twentieth century a way was found of using the brightness of Cepheids to measure distances in space.*

COBE satellite *The Cosmic Background Explorer satellite, launched on November 18, 1989. Its sensitive instruments recorded slight differences in the cosmic background radiation. These were said to represent structures in the very early universe that led to the formation of clusters of galaxies.*

Comet *A relatively small object traveling around the sun in a long, stretched-out orbit. Comets are thought to be "dirty snowballs" about a half mile (one kilometer) across. When a comet gets near the sun a tail forms from gas and dust as part of the comet boils off into space. The tail may be 6 million miles (10 million kilometers) long.*

Cosmic background radiation *The faint radiation left over from the big bang explosion. This radiation comes from all points of the sky.*

Cosmological constant *A factor introduced into his equations by Albert Einstein to balance the force of gravity and ensure that the universe would neither expand nor contract.*

Cosmology *The study of the origin, evolution and nature of the universe.*

Dark matter *Matter in the universe that cannot be detected by our scientific instruments. Some scientists have suggested that there must be more material in the universe than we can see and that some of it is in the form of invisible dark matter.*

Eclipse *An eclipse occurs when light from one object passes through the shadow of another object and is temporarily blocked from view. An eclipse of the sun occurs when the shadow of the moon falls on part of the Earth and hides the sun.*

Electron *A tiny particle, smaller than an atom. Electrons are found in all atoms and also as free electrons unattached to anything.*

Ellipse *A geometric figure like a flattened circle.*

Epicycle *A small circle, the center of which rolls around a larger circle.*

Focus *One of two points on the long axis of an ellipse. The sum of the distances from any point on the ellipse to each focus is always the same.*

Fundamental essence *An idea put forward by the Greek philosopher Anaximander. This was the mysterious substance from which all other materials in the universe came.*

Galaxy *A huge assembly of trillions of stars, gas and dust held together by gravity.*

Globular cluster *A spherical collection of between 10,000 and a million stars.*

Gravitational force *The force that acts between any two objects in the universe, attracting them to each other.*

Gravity *The phenomenon associated with the gravitational force acting on an object. The weight of an object is determined by the force of gravity acting on it.*

Great Wall *The name given to a vast chain of galaxies extending over 500 million light-years, first discovered in 1990.*

Inflationary model *Inflation is a theory of the origin of the universe that suggests that shortly after the big bang there was a brief period, lasting a tiny fraction of a second, during which the universe expanded at a colossal rate. In the course of this inflationary period enormous amounts of energy were produced.*

Interference *Interference occurs when two or more waves pass through each other. Where the waves cross they add their energy together. If the crest of one wave coincides with the trough of another they cancel each other out. If two crests coincide they add to give a wave crest that is twice as big. Interference patterns show us where the waves are adding and where they are canceling. We can see this in the ripples produced when two stones are dropped simultaneously into a pond.*

Inverse-square law *A law in which the size of a force is determined by the square of the distance from the source of the force. If you triple the distance the force is reduced to a ninth, and if you halve the distance the force increases four times.*

LGM *Little Green Men. This term jokingly refers to the life that probably exists elsewhere in the universe, possibly taken from science fiction references to "little green men from Mars."*

Light-year *The distance light travels through free space in one year. It is equivalent to 5.878 trillion miles (9.46 trillion kilometers).*

Meteor *A streak of light in the night sky caused by a rocky particle from space glowing white hot through friction as it enters the Earth's atmosphere. A meteor big enough to pass through the atmosphere and strike the surface is called a meteorite.*

Microwave radiation *Radiation that is similar to other forms of radiation, such as light waves and radio waves. Microwaves are longer than light waves, but shorter than radio waves. The cosmic background radiation is detected as microwaves.*

Nebula *Originally used to describe any fuzzy area of light visible through a telescope, this term is now used for huge clouds of gas and dust between the stars.*

Neutron star *A star that has used up all its nuclear fuel and collapsed so much that its atomic particles have been crushed together. If it collapsed any further it would form a black hole.*

Nova *A star that becomes over a thousand times brighter in a period of a few days. Novas are believed to be caused in double-star systems when material is transferred from one star to another, resulting in a titanic thermonuclear explosion.*

Paradox *A paradox is a situation that doesn't make sense or goes against what we believe to be true or possible.*

Parallax *The apparent movement of a distant object against a more distant background when viewed from two different positions.*

Primordial atom *A cosmic "super-atom" suggested by Georges Lemaître as being the starting point of the universe. The primordial atom is supposed to have exploded in the big bang. Primordial means "existing at the beginning."*

Pulsar *An object far out in space that produces regular pulses of radiation. Pulsars are believed to be rapidly spinning neutron stars.*

Radiation *Energy that travels in the form of waves, such as light, microwaves and radio waves. Radiation may also mean a stream of high-energy atomic particles, such as electrons.*

Radio astronomy *The study of objects in space by detecting the radio waves they give off rather than visible light.*

Radio waves *A form of low-energy radiation. Radio waves behave in a similar way to light waves, but they are very much longer and special equipment is needed to detect them.*

Ripples *The faint disturbances in the cosmic background radiation detected by the COBE satellite were sometimes referred to as ripples, in the same way as we might refer to ripples on the smooth surface of a pond. Cosmic ripples may show places where the big bang explosion was not quite even.*

They are unbelievably vast structures. Some are so big that the universe is not yet old enough for light to have crossed them.

Satellite *A small body in space that orbits a larger one. The moon is a satellite of the Earth and the Earth is a satellite of the sun.*

Singularity *An infinitely small, infinitely dense point where the laws of physics no longer apply. No one knows what might happen in a singularity: matter, energy, space and time may be destroyed, or created. The entire universe may have exploded out from a singularity in the big bang.*

Steady state *The name given to a theory put forward by Fred Hoyle, which states that the universe has no beginning and no end and maintains much the same appearance. To account for the fact that the universe is expanding, the steady state theory says that new matter is continually being created from space.*

Velocity *Velocity usually means the same thing as speed, but in scientific terms a velocity is given by the speed of an object and the direction in which it is traveling.*

Voids *Vast volumes of empty space hundreds of light-years across.*

Ylem *The name given by George Gamow to the matter that he suggested existed in the early universe. It was made up of atomic particles in a sea of radiation.*

Index

WITHDRAWN